Greatness Finds a Way

FACING THE PAST TO EMBRACE THE FUTURE

DR. ELENA SHERWOOD

First Printing: 2021
ALANNA RUSNAK PUBLISHING
ISBN: 978-1-990336-07-2

Alanna Rusnak Publishing
282906 Normanby/Bentinck Townline
Durham, Ontario, Canada, N0G 1R0

www.alannarusnakpublishing.com

Cover photograph by Elizabeth & Jane Photography

For my three rocket scientists.

For you I couldn't help, here's why.

For you I could, here's why.

And for the people I will help, this is why.

Foreword

When I was invited to provide the foreword for *Greatness Finds a Way*, I agreed, trusting there would be layers to the writing, a baring of the soul, and honest experiences that resonated with me. Elena and I were in the same PhD cohort so I had a number of opportunities to read her academic work and to learn from her insights. Our shared time together gave me an academic colleague and a dear friend whose courage has always inspired.

I started skimming to get a general gist but very quickly into the read, I realized that I needed to sit down in a comfy place and lose myself in what she had to share. It was something so deep and profound. I am grateful.

Readers of *Greatness Finds a Way* shall discover, as I did, that Elena's story of immigration and the hurt that comes when a child is left behind allows the reader to walk alongside her as she relives those experiences. Together, readers and the author find healing while sharing some of life's universal truths of injustice, family demands, and the roles all adults play in the lives of children.

As Elena's book reveals, we are shaped not only by those closest to us, but also by chance meetings and deep connections sustained perhaps because of a deep primordial energy that burns within each of us. In her writing, the parent-child relationship, the ways children protect themselves, and the flawed adult these experiences form allows the reader to see into their own life-mirror while simultaneously grieving and celebrating the author's story. This is soul touching, hopeful work.

Here's to crispy fish skin and all that life brings us. "Greatness finds a way."

Yasmin Dean, PhD, RSW
Associate Professor | Social Work
Chair | Department of Child Studies and Social Work
Mount Royal University, Mohkinstsis/Calgary

GREATNESS FINDS A WAY

DR. ELENA SHERWOOD

2021

Introduction

Perhaps a story begins the second we realize there is one to be told. This is what brings me before you today; it isn't perfect and it isn't pretty, but it is full of lessons I sincerely hope will help you tell your own.

For as long as I can remember, elusive thoughts drifted in the undercurrents of my awareness. They were undefined and unsettling. I moved forward by setting a goal on top of them. Chasing after those distractions took centerstage, blocking everything else, and it felt like winning.

Goal.

Chase.

Achieve.

Repeat.

Easy enough? No. None of it was easy, but it let me dwell where I preferred to be: far from the thoughts that weighed me down. I sought and welcomed the mental escape. I depended on it.

It turns out we can only run so far from ourselves. The thoughts we try to leave behind always resurface. Lately they have been doing just that, coming back up. Again, I set my goal maker on it. I decided to face those thoughts head on, to harness those bad boys and set them free—set *me* free.

Something big happened: instead of clearing my mind, I *awakened* it. It is the awakened me who writes to you. It seems my healing won't be complete until the lessons are used to help others. So I begin.

Somewhere in this book, whether on the back cover or in the 'about the author' section, it's noted that I'm a therapist. I'm a good one. I've done a lot to earn that statement. I "see" people's sacred selves, the ones they lock away because that's how they've learned to protect themselves. What I've yet to see on a book cover, however, is emphasis on the fact the author is a mere human, walking in shoes like yours, wearing clothes like you wear, no greater, higher, or better than you. Because we are not. *I* am not.

Envision a middle-aged woman tucked under a blanket on the couch, a rom-com in front of her, and a full bag of Flaming Hot Cheetos with Lime on her lap. She is at the mercy of the pancaked lacklustre heroine, preparing for the "shocking" final scene by grabbing a root beer. That is who speaks to you here. A woman. A human. A mortal with Cheeto stained fingers.

I am humbly inviting you to come a bit closer and walk with me. I have so much to tell you. I am not merely extending my hand; I'm reaching out from my soul to yours.

I'm not in love with my own story but it's mine, and it is full of things remarkably like yours, of that I'm certain. I need to travel through it, and I need your worthy company to do it justice so I tell it truthfully. It might not seem clear yet, but this book is really for you. You'll learn from all this that though we haven't met, I know your story, and you'll know that I know you're out there. I know what you've been through, or are going through, and you are not alone. You and I are more alike than we are different.

This book isn't about the storytelling. It's about the message: greatness finds a way. Always. We all have greatness within us. You, me, everybody. Greatness wants us to soar, because we are meant to. WE. ARE. MEANT. TO. You already know this. But maybe you don't know you know it. Your greatness brought you here to gain new insight and lead you to sustainable fruition. I'm so proud of you for that!

In more ways than you know, your greatness has already found a way. If you "I Spy" your way through your own life the way I will within these pages for the entire world to see (God help me), you will recognize your own story reflected. You will see *your* strength, *your* resilience, and the fortitude that reveals *your* greatness; perhaps you will also see the circumstances that shaped you, how they lined up in such a perfect way to grow you into the person you're meant to be.

Ready? Let's do this!

CHAPTER ONE

Sorrow begins when our desires fail to manifest.

Let me begin with a moment that is seared into my memory. I stood in an echoey room, four years old, barefoot on the granite-like floor in our house in Manila. I faced the stairwell leading to the bedrooms upstairs, over which loomed a statue of Jesus encased in glass, his heart wrapped in thorns. It was midday, the safest time to look up. In the kitchen, someone fried fish. My mouth watered in anticipation of the salty meal I would soon enjoy. I inhaled the scent and listened for the light spatter of oil. Everything seemed perfect.

Maybe I'll get some of the crispy skin today, the tastiest part, a crunchy bite or two, I thought.

We'll see. That's what my mother said when I asked for something and there was no real answer. "We'll see."

I looked down at my faded shorts, once orange, now like the flesh of a pale peach. They were elastic waisted, the front seam slanted way off to the side. As I straightened them, I wished they were pink, the really pretty kind. Pretty pink, unlike this one, passed down by three others before me. My head stayed low and my heart sank along with it.

The truth settled on my young shoulders, weighing me down. There would be no crispy fish skin for me. The best parts are always for others. There would be no pink or pretty. There just wouldn't be.

In that moment, I felt terribly alone. Something inside me ached. Sopping, heavy sadness. It lasted only a moment, but long enough to leave an impression of the scar. When you were one of six children in a staunchly Catholic, patriarchal family like mine, there was only the obeying and the following. You had no voice. You were invisible. That's just how it was.

Two big questions here: can one feel cold to the bone standing on the edge of the equator and, can one feel terribly lonely in the company of so many? Yes, and hell yes.

I look back now and I see hints of spiritedness. Even with that internal ache—which came and went from time to time—I loved everyone in the magical way a child can. Oh, how I loved them all! One sister drew me paper dolls to cut out and play with, another painted my name on a rock so I'd always know how to spell it. I treasured my name stone. I felt joy! I celebrated my solitary pink dress. I was teased for over-wearing it, but it was precious to me. I followed anyone around who would let me, and I watched in awe as my mother sewed me a dress from leftover garments. I loved standing around when she was at that Singer, listening to the hum of creation. Such things she made! I celebrated so much, I searched and found moments and things that filled my life. I was a lucky, special little girl.

I was eight years old when the process of our immigration to Canada began. My family was divided in two as my mother and the three oldest children went ahead. The rest of us were to follow. *Soon*, we were told. I was in the latter group, left behind. *I was left behind.* People leave and come back all the time, but this day felt different. On this day, it was hard to breathe.

Whenever I think of that fateful afternoon at Manila International, no matter how many years pass and how many times I tell the story, the sharpness of that moment comes back. It is upon me in spades as I write.

Dialects, Tagalog, street vendors with souvenirs, and peanuts with extra fried garlic filled the humid spaces. Some of us had ice cream as we waited for the departure. I nursed my strawberry cone as I studied my mother, the most beautiful woman I'd ever seen. She wore a deep blue custom-tailored pantsuit, sewn specifically for this day, topped with a necklace of baby shells and carefully styled hair.

When the time came for goodbyes there were hardly any. It felt casual, though everything within me cried out for a scene. *This is happening,* I thought. Etched in my mind, perhaps my clearest memory of all, are my mother's lovely curls, moving away until indistinguishable in the bustling sea of black and grey heads. She didn't turn around. I held my breath, waiting for her to turn, but she did not look back.

The car ride home was dark and silent, invaded only by traffic lights, the humming air-conditioner, and the clicking noise of the Renault's turn signal. Wordlessly, my father stopped and picked up a Robinson's barbecued chicken, a rare treat for us when we were complete. *When we were complete.* The enticing fragrance disoriented me. The way my heartache blended with the promised enjoyment of that savoury, juicy, roasted poultry wrapped in foil with the logo on one side felt like betrayal. Why did he buy the chicken? To comfort? Distract? No. It was *to make us forget that the single most important figure in our lives just flew away on a Pan American Airways flight to the other side of the world and we didn't know when we'd see her again.*

Pain made food tasteless. I was left with no choice, so I swallowed both.

No one told me that was the last time I'd see the mother I remembered, and no one told me "soon" would last five very long years.

Any therapist—no, every *person* alive—would tout the importance of the mother and child bond, sibling connections, and all that jazz. I look back now as a trained adult and feel a lump in my throat. I salute little me for staying intact and remaining a hopeful child during my motherless years.

I focused my affection on my father, remaining siblings, and the extended family who collectively raised us. We sold the big house, lived in an apartment until the new one was built, and then settled in several months later. My father threw himself into his work, my sister and I played in the streets with new friends wherever we lived, and my grades were solid.

When I processed this as an adult, my own therapist pointed out that I lost both my parents at the same time. She was right. It is astounding what humans can endure, with so little, under so much. Parts of it were hard. I could handle the sadness of not having a parent at school events, but not the embarrassment and humiliation. It crushed me. I didn't sign up for anything that would draw attention to my situation, even when I longed to: track and field (I was told I'd do well in it), team sports, group dance performances, anything. Invisibility during those times hurt less.

Fast forward five years (why it took this long wasn't ever clarified, hard as I fought for answers), we reunited at what was then called Toronto International. On a cold December afternoon, specks of dust fell from the heavens—not at all what I imagined snow would look like—and I received a warm "Welcome to Canada!" handshake from the tall white customs officer at the airport, but nowhere else.

There were no tears, no real conversations, no emotions of any kind. My mother appeared sharpened, her shoulders and chin more pointed and defined, her voice scratchier and less steady than I remembered as she spoke in soft strained tones. She put a neck brace on as soon as we reached her car and I wondered if she was in pain. We climbed into her green Nova, defrost stickers peeling away from the back window. I would learn later that she'd been ill several times in the five years we'd been separated.

There was no picking up where we left off, there was no connection from past to present. I was as alone and unheard as I'd been when I was four and eight, more so now, because I was suddenly a thirteen-year-old irritant. Nothing I did or didn't do made me less so. The routine was the same. School. Cook. Do dishes. Church. We brought a giant wooden rosary with us from the Philippines that we hung on the wall. Every Filipino I knew had made or at least owned a hand version, mine had been with pink translucent beads. I wondered why I no longer found comfort in this favourite religious item.

I didn't have permission to be honest with my feelings; no one spoke or acknowledged they existed. All matters of my heart remained within, ignored and disregarded, so there they stayed. My parents sought work for my father. Bills had to be paid and food put on the table. The house was kept cool to save money, expenses were kept to a minimum. The objective was to survive.

Early teens are about defining one's identity. I lost my country, my language, and the feeling of "home" all in one fell swoop, so resilient me got busy adapting *again*. I ditched my accent (which was disturbingly easy). I didn't do it to shuck off my culture, but to increase the likelihood of being heard somewhere, elsewhere, anywhere. Accents were ridiculed in my small school, immigrants regarded with condescension, and I had no interest in being different. I must have known that whatever I would need in life would come from the world outside my house. In time my world expanded, I made great friends as I'd done several times before. In fact, I found a glorious blend of characters who still delight me today.

Even now, I can't make sense of the years that followed. Every adaptive goal I achieved was either ignored or misread, then thwarted. In seventh grade—the year I arrived—the volleyball coach saw potential in my skill and offered me a spot on the school team. My parents didn't allow it. They said it interfered with school. I was proud of the strides I'd made in establishing friendships, but my parents reigned in my social world by scanning every one of my actions with a scrutinizing and disappointed eye. Kids invited me to church dances, cottages, and fun activities, but these were met with a ready no. I settled in and loved my newly built Catholic high school. For the first time in my life, I had a strong social network I wouldn't have to leave.

When tuition was imposed two years later, my parents demanded I move to the rundown, underfunded public high school across from our home even though I had the money from my cashier job to pay for it. It was free and barely a block over, they'd said. The dense outdoor smoking area was visible from our window. In my gut, I sensed that it wasn't at all about the money or location. They hoped to pry me away from the kind young man who'd started calling our house and now they found a means to do it; for added measure, they declared a no dating rule.

The hardest thing to process, even today, was the effort with which they stifled the very qualities that were uniquely me. I was empathic, intuitive, curious, expressive, and determined, yet they found these grating. No one noticed that I'd done well through monumental changes in the absence of real parents. Wounds like these can leave one constantly seeking validation, which is what happened for me.

Refusing to be defeated, resilient me learned to lie. I learned how to sneak off to meet my boyfriend because he loved me. I refused to live without the first person who made me feel worthy. It was real. In that time and place, my teenage love was, in fact, the truest thing in my life. Someone cared about my feelings, enjoyed and genuinely desired my company. In fact, he'd gone to great lengths to tell me so with cards, gifts, and acts of kindness.

Of course, the ways of the young are fickle, and when the relationship ended unexpectedly a year later, the break-up ignited all the other pain I'd hidden from. Not surprising. I only knew that it was the darkest time I'd ever endured; a cloud settles upon me now as I revisit that grief. After days —maybe weeks—of intermittent sobbing, my grades were in danger; so, I lay down my sorrow and stood up. Again. This time I learned a valuable lesson: I realized I could only control my own behaviour, and I could only rely on myself. A sobering thought for a seventeen-year-old girl.

I studied harder and began to think of my future. My ex-boyfriend was seen at the movies with a pretty girl. She was everything I wasn't: tall, blonde, outgoing, and free to spend as much time with him as they both pleased. To add to the sting of feeling discarded and less than, she walked the halls of my dumpy high school for me to either see or avoid. I sunk my head and broken heart into schoolwork. I raised my marks.

My lost beloved came back with genuine regret and undying love several weeks later. I'd like to say that I told him no, that I deserved someone who'd never leave me, someone who'd never look elsewhere, someone who would give me his entire heart, exclusively and always. But I couldn't. I chose the easiest road out of pain because taking him back hurt less. Finding ways to escape, or at least dull my pain was a honed skill by then. We dated for a couple more years until our lives led us down divergent paths.

CHAPTER TWO

Sometimes, all you need is you.

I am thankful for the moments my inner strength emerged and took over. It's as if I knew, somewhere deep inside, that a fuller life was possible. In my final year of high school, as I flipped through the glossy Ryerson calendar my sister brought me, my heart stopped when I saw a gateway in two words: Social Worker. I read the description. The entry requirements made me wince. *Yikes!* It would be tight. I dropped the flyer and rushed to the guidance office.

"That program is too hard for you," the counsellor said.

As if that naysayer could stop me. *Bigger forces have tried, jerk*, I thought to myself. I demanded the paperwork, then travelled an hour and a half to the institution's admission desk.

By the skin of my teeth, several months later, I got into the program.

I had no choice but to drive my inner engine hard, working evenings, weekends, and summers to pay every penny. To save money I lived at home for the first year. I used the commuting time to get caught up on readings. I made good friends at both school and work, places that were far more pleasant to spend time in.

I craved a space of my own so, during my second year, I lived alone. Unfortunately, the only place I could afford was a dark and dingy basement in a seedy part of Toronto. A murder took place two doors down from me on the week I moved in, but I didn't care. It was cozy enough and within my budget.

I visited home once in a while. A few months after I'd moved out, my mother drove me back after a Sunday meal, and it was the first time she saw my apartment.

It was nighttime. My small door was down a dark alley and through a leaning garage. When we got inside my mother stood in silence, observing the place. I'd stripped my bed to wash the one fitted sheet I owned, exposing the used mattress I'd wrapped in garbage bags because I questioned its sanitary condition.

My mother took it all in: saggy twin, black plastic, sparse furniture, an empty fridge, half a pink shower liner cut crookedly to be a bathroom door, the other half for the precarious shower itself. The sack of rice they'd given me was near empty, as was the jumbo pack of toilet paper, also from them.

She stood quietly. She swallowed hard. I didn't know her well then and didn't understand her expression. Today I know what it was: sheer heartbreak. She didn't stay long.

Because of the distance between us, I didn't understand the gravity of her phone call the following day. She spoke in a hushed, shaky voice. "I'll help you with rent so you can get a better place," she said. There were many things I couldn't (or wouldn't) hear or see then, so her words were met with light dismissal. "No thank you, I'm doing all right."

The offer of money could have been many things: an apology of sorts for leaving me; an attempt at nurturance; kindness; an effort to make amends; an acceptance of her part in the rift between us; or sorrow over how far I'd go and how poorly I was willing to live to avoid staying under their roof. Perhaps all of the above. Unfortunately, I was certain it would come with conditions and control, so I held my ground. She didn't push and never offered again.

For the remaining years of school, I acquiesced to the convenience and affordability of living with roommates. It was a sound decision and life-long relationships were formed: one would later be my maid of honour, and others anchors during the weathered times in decades to come.

The years sped up, and the long-anticipated graduation day finally arrived.

I finished my degree without owing one cent. I found a vocation that thirsted for my gifts. I accepted a job offer well before I was even done school. I found my world, my people, and my voice. I found a life that was my very own. I was free!

On that brilliant sunny day, I stood in my blue and white gown, vibrating with positive energy, well-blended with the masses lined up outside the auditorium. I saw my parents come through the barricade. They spotted me instantly and offered gentle waves. My mother wore a pastel dress which she smoothed uncomfortably, never a fan of social events outside the church. She held her head high that day; her shoulders looked relaxed, and I saw a touch of make-up along with her trademark curls. My father seemed taller than his five foot five inches, dapper in his dark grey suit and red tie. His oversized camera hung around his neck. Some things glinted in the sun. Tie clip. Cuff links.

My father used a whole role of film that day. They let me choose a restaurant despite the cost and I chose Red Lobster. As we waited for the meal, engulfed in the blessed aroma of garlic butter and seafood, my mother pulled a small box from her red, purposeful nylon purse. She placed it before me.

I opened it slowly to find a diamond ring: a small stone set on a gold circle on a gold band.

My mother told of how my father picked it out himself, from the vast collection at that jewelry place in our favourite outlet mall. "Oh, I miss that mall," I told her. And then to my father, "Did you, really?"

He was famous for his bright smiles, but that wasn't the one he wore in that moment. This one was subdued, a shy grin with meaningful eye contact. "Of course," he said softly. It became the most precious thing I owned, more sacred than the rock with my name in childhood, which had lost its lustre. It still sits permanently on my finger.

It was an unforgettable day

CHAPTER THREE

A glimmer of hope is hope nonetheless.

Being alive and feeling alive are two vastly different things. It didn't matter that life was better after I graduated because I didn't feel it. I kept going. Constantly pushing forward was my default setting. *I could not stop.* Somewhere along the way, feeling at odds with the world, with life, and with myself, became habit. The consequences of surviving my first two decades, then the first several years of living independently, took their toll. My steady and rewarding job emptied me. I anticipated trouble and found fault. I searched for it. However, even in my state, I forged and kept solid friendships. The ability to *be* with others was one of the things I kept regardless of my complex family life. Not only did I get better at connecting, but it was also one of the powerful forces that got me to the other side.

I say this because not long after graduating I fell deeply in love, and this man changed the dynamic of my life thereafter. We had been friends for years until a series of events unfolded to bring us closer, and then, there was no desire to turn back. I didn't understand how being half of this relationship made me feel whole, as if I could do anything simply because this person closest to my heart believed I could. Truth be told, I was terrified and questioned everything. What if this, like many things I'd needed before, would be taken from me too? What if I failed and pushed him away? What if he saw the real me and ran scared? My parents didn't approve because he was white, he was joining the military, and worse yet, he was *Protestant*. While their views were inconsequential to me, all of it still had to be managed.

What if he lets me down the way my parents did?

Could the universe be so cruel?

It was not. It was gloriously rewarding and generous. This man would become my husband of thirty years, and the father of my now adult sons. We were a perfect match: my gift was the ability to reach out openly and relentlessly, and his was the ability to decidedly stay. The limits of our gifts would be tested several times.

As I've laid out so far in this story, loved ones up to this point had mostly ignored, abandoned, forgotten, silenced, or crushed me. (I listed those as impersonally as a grocery list: milk, sugar, and eggs. I acknowledge them without feeling them.) But there were feelings underneath, and they were intensely personal. The cumulative pain made everything hurt. How fortuitous it was that I didn't know how truly cold and alone I'd been until I was with him.

For the first time in my life, I had a real home. Home was sometimes in a hotel room where we met to spare us both a six-hour drive when he was in training. It was in handwritten letters or a long-awaited phone call. I only knew that I cherished us, often praying, "*Oh God, please, please I beg you, please don't send me back out there again to that place of feeling deeply alone. Please. No more.*"

I will always shed a tear for my young self and how far she made it on her own. Though I tried to ignore the wounds that weren't yet scars of my youth, they were always there under the surface. It felt like slow stabs with a big knife that eventually reached my core.

I wish I could say that love was enough in our early years of marriage. I only knew to keep pushing forward, at all costs, and with the stakes rising, I kicked it up a few notches as I fought for us. I conjured up a life plan: marriage, a master's degree, a house, and two children. I also wanted the best job with the best hours, the best pay, and the best working conditions. I can't tell you how distressing it is for me to revisit that mindset today. My chest constricts just thinking about it. I held everything in my life so tightly, perhaps as destructively as my parents hung on to me. I learned their fear. I embodied it. I was far from okay and the scary part was, I didn't know it.

I got busy ticking things off my list but whenever I was forced to pause, the chaos of my thoughts engulfed me. *Keep going. Move. Get it done. While you're there do this too. Do more, MORE!*

Goal.

Chase.

Achieve.

Repeat.

It helped to have someone who believed in the goodness of me just as I was, the only problem was that I didn't believe him, at least not in the matters that concerned me.

Our first five years were a blur as we both established careers. My husband's work took us to the remote northern community of Cold Lake,

Alberta, immersing him in stresses of his own. He carried out his career with as much commitment and dedication I afforded mine. I had known nothing of this culture. I would later learn its challenges. I simply pushed forward, smothering unsettled thoughts with a master's degree and the pursuit of the so-called perfect job. Being with clients in a therapy room got easier the further away I got from myself. I ignored unsettled thoughts repeatedly.

Until I became a mother.

Nothing about having a child went as planned. It took a while to get pregnant, I ballooned with weight, and my son was born two weeks past his due date after twenty-four hours of labour and an emergency C-section.

In my hospital room, twelve hours post-surgery, beneath a stark clean sheet and cotton mesh blanket, emotions overwhelmed me. The snow fell slowly outside the window. I watched with vigilance. My husband sat on a poly-blend orange chair with a tired maple frame. He held our soft, blue-toqued bundle whose eyes were squeezed shut, mouth wide open, pausing as he committed to yet another full-bodied, high-pitched wail. And there it was. My husband soothed and rocked him, unaware I was stifling a cry that would match my newborn's, because suddenly, out of nowhere, loneliness punched me hard.

My mind couldn't reconcile the clash of beauty and heartache. I was back in the Renault, the smell of barbecue chicken surrounding me again. This time it was a hundred times worse, because it was all my fault. All. Mine. I pushed us to have this baby. I wanted him so badly, but now this tender fragile being, with the most precious little heartbeat, encased in his barrel-chested torso, had me for a mother: unworthy, undeserving, and broken. I was selfish and ego-centred for needing him.

I knew I wouldn't be enough. I knew I'd never be. There was no possible way I could be the kind of mother I knew he needed and deserved.

Yet I wanted him, and I had him anyway.

I prayed that someday he would find enough mercy in that precious heart to forgive me.

Somewhere in his late teens my son and I would stand in the kitchen, an island between us. It would be several provinces away from that hospital, and several stages of our lives later. I would feel brave, watching him pour chocolate milk into a tall, water-stained glass. I would blurt out an incomprehensible, all-encompassing apology. It would be for all my maternal shortcomings, all the endless moments I couldn't be what he needed. The emotional tirades I unleashed upon him over nothing. For all the things I failed at. For the many ways I will yet fall short.

He would pause mid-pour and look up. He would direct his dark eyes at me in confusion and declare, "Whaaat? What are talking about? I have the best parents in the world. You and dad are so good at it, I find it hard to believe you were ever anything else." He would let me hug him, allowing a couple more seconds because he's kind that way. Then he would smile that killer smirk, pick up his drink, and walk away, pausing only to grab the Oreos from the top cupboard. I would watch him open the door to descend to his man cave and close it ever so gently behind him.

From there, I would find the corner in my closet and sit. I would wrap my arms tightly around my knees, bury my head in them, and release the long-stifled cry I'd held in for nearly twenty years. *Relief.* Emotion would pour onto my favourite blue plaid shirt. I would whisper a prayer: *To all that is good and light, God Almighty, I thank you for this sacred moment. My son survived me.*

I have two children. They are just under three years apart, and while the arrival of my second son wasn't nearly as difficult (a scheduled C-section), other things posed challenges. My husband's job took him away more often and with less and less notice. Had I eased my death grip on my career and parked it for an extended maternity break, our lives would have been easier, but I couldn't. Two weeks before I was to go back to work, I had cause to reflect.

I was reaching for the last item in the dishwasher, a purple, well-chewed, sippy cup lid. It should have been replaced long before. *Some mother I am,* I thought, *feeding my child plastic.* I detested those cups, and I never found an easy way to wash and keep track of the clear piece that attaches inside, and I couldn't find it then. *How many have I lost?* Another failure. I added that to the endless list of things I couldn't do. I couldn't buy more cups or automatically wash them. I couldn't do it all. It felt like I couldn't do anything. Emotions slowly rose and I found myself clutching the speckled pressed wood counter. It was sticky. *Of course it's sticky,* I thought. This last, *I can't even wipe up messes,* pushed me over. I rested my whole upper body on the structure, head buried under my arms. I struggled to breathe. In. Out. Steady. Try again.

Something was terribly wrong. It was time to get help.

I've had two therapists in my lifetime. This is when I met the first. She was kind, she listened, and she concluded that going back to work was about loss. She surmised that I'd experienced a lot of loss given my history, and after two sessions I thanked her and told her I was fine. I didn't tell her that whenever my husband walked out our front door with his back to me, leaving for another work trip, the visual of his dark head walking away cut me up inside. I didn't tell her that I couldn't risk losing my career because I didn't trust the universe to let me keep him, so I always needed a way to support my babies. I didn't tell her how much I loved my children, and how it broke my heart that they deserved so much more than me for a mother.

I'm baffled by how oblivious I was of my own mental state, because there were clues. I saw my doctor for unrelated reasons and out of nowhere he recommended I take some time off work and wrote out two things: one was a referral for counselling, the other was a prescription for anti-depressants. On the way to my car, I ripped the first one and fisted it into a ball, tossing it in the lined mesh bin: a three pointer. After a meaningful pause, I drove to my pharmacist. I trusted and valued the words of my physician (aside from the counselling recommendation, of course), so I resigned myself to at least take the damn drugs.

CHAPTER FOUR

The universe is a masterful manager.

Several months later, a bittersweet encounter changed the trajectory of my life. A new coworker joined my work team, a woman with reddish blond waves and a refreshing South African accent. She was an encouraging soul and a complete joy to be around. She was older than me and an easy friend. She liked rooibos tea, and her laugh and smile came directly from her heart.

When we first met, there were two reasons she caught me off guard: her name was Elsa, my mother's name and, without a moment's hesitation, she came at me with a warm, all-encompassing hug. My relationship with my mother was better by then but still complex.

A few days after her arrival, this new friend paused outside my office, standing still until I looked up to face her. I can still hear her exact words echo through my head today—lilts, tone, and all—as clear as that magnificent moment seventeen years ago. "Elena, why aren't you doing your PhD? You are so smart and competent!" This dear kind lady had her doctorate, lived my version of a dream career, including giving advice on a live radio show. The thought of her always warms my heart.

"You are lovely. Thank you, but no." I said. "My life is hard enough. Between my husband's career, my job, and our young boys, I'm barely making it as is."

Without batting a pleasantly pale eyelash she responded, "Ahhck, Elaaayna! Life is hard no matter what. You may as well do what you really love! Your kids are adaptable."

She carried on down the hall and my heart ached as I sat in silence. A lump formed in my throat. I closed my sturdy government-issue door and turned the lock until it clicked reassuringly. The thickness in my throat felt like something was pooling there and it had to be released.

Tears came. They were soundless and guttural. I was disoriented and confused; my chest tightened. Does the universe have a sick sense of humour? Why would it send me this blessing of a person with the name of the woman who birthed me? Why would it dangle before me—nay, shove upon my face—the kind of life I wanted and craved when I'd always known those great things are meant for others? *Always. ALWAYS.* Just like the crispy fish skin, the pretty pink clothes, (no amount of pink in my adult wardrobe assuaged the longings of my childhood) and the attentive mothers. They weren't for me. I got lucky with my husband, but the rest would never be mine.

The ache went deeper as the devastating reality hit: my life would have been so much easier, happier, fuller, and more joyful had this wonderful lady—the bearer of my mother's name—*been* my mother.

Several weeks later, fate began to reveal its hand. Two days before Christmas my husband was called away. Likely for two weeks, he told me.

We were powerless to stop it, that was military life. Our marriage was stable but distant. I'd tired of unpredictability well before that day, but this, having our Christmas taken from us? It was all we had. We needed it to reconnect. We needed it more than anything.

Losing it was my *undoing*.

I handled the situation. I orchestrated an earlier Christmas morning. I pulled out the beautiful down jacket I'd ordered for my husband months before. I wanted to surprise him. There was no time to wrap it, and I choked back the anger over the gifting moment I was denied. I shamelessly hinted to a friend that we'd be alone. Out of kindness she invited us to join their big meal.

During the lull of Boxing Day, I took the boys for pizza. The friendly waitress chatted, and my older son said, "Santa had to come to our house *before* Christmas 'cause Daddy was going away."

This heavenly creature, this angel with an apron, glanced at me in support and understanding. She sensed I was barely holding it together, and she looked at my son, leaned in towards him and said, "Wow! He came to our house early too, aren't we special?"

I found myself nearing tears at the generosity of her heart. I wonder where the human race would be without simple acts of kindness. I gave her a grateful smile which she acknowledged gracefully. Later, I left her a very big tip.

That night, as soon as the boys were tucked in, I fired up my old Hewlett Packard and rolled my squeaky, slightly unbalanced chair up to the desk. It was time. This was it. I searched. My fingers flew across the keyboard. It didn't take long until I burst out loud, "Aha! There you are!" I clicked away, printed, and wrote. The minutes turned into hours; it was just about midnight when I finished.

I did it.

I completed the doctoral program application. I did it in one sitting, and sent it back out into the universe with a silent wish and soulful prayer. *Please, please give me this one.*

Once again, I'd taken control of my life. I thought of my husband and somehow knew we'd make this work. We had to. His career hadn't broken us, I hoped mine wouldn't either.

Several months later I would receive my admission letter with an accompanying scholarship. My husband would move us to Calgary and drive sixteen hours a weekend to be with us. I would live on coffee and knowledge, make life-long friends, push my academic mind well beyond what I believed possible, and do it all while caring for a pre-schooler and first grader.

I would finish a six-year degree in less than four.

Donned in the rental blue, red, and yellow cap and gown reserved only for PhD grads, I would stand proudly on a stage, shakily accepting my parchment. My face would feel warm, as if the sun cast a ray of sunshine upon me that kept pace with all my movements. I would feel like a million bucks. I would look out at the crowd and my heart would still when I see my husband—the man who never draws attention to himself—stand to his fullest six-foot frame in a sea of those seated around him, clapping with all his might, beaming! He and the boys would meet me with flowers.

My delightful South African friend would fly in for this glorious occasion. A handful of dear friends would pause their own lives, travel from afar to share this day.

I would, perhaps for the very first time, truly, at least right then, believe I'm capable and loved.

CHAPTER FIVE

Grief is a compass.

T he years in grad school were rocky, at best. The workload and demands were steady. Only six months into the program, I got a call to get on a plane: my mother had lost consciousness, likely from an aneurism, and was in a coma. She was on life support until all the children could come.

To say goodbye.

There was no hope. She only had a few days at best.

Amidst the beeps in the ICU, there was only her and I for a tender moment. I held her hand. It was warm. A hose of sorts was taped to her mouth to hold it in, her bottom lip visibly lopsided.

There were two things I knew with certainty: that she loved God, and that she loved us all in the best ways she could, *deeply*. Her life hadn't been easy. She said prayers three times a day, and as sure as the morning sun, I was always in them. I'd called her from time to time when I needed her prayers. She stopped telling me to talk to God myself and instead accepted every request. "You always land on your feet," she said during each call or visit, with a slight catch in her throat. Was it sorrow or regret she felt then? No, I know it was *pride*.

I watched her chest rise and fall. She had used her old-style curl rollers recently. I wondered if she slept with them on. I never asked. Two curls framed her remarkably youthful skin. At seventy-two, she didn't look a day over fifty. Olay can't do that, it's genetics. With great care around the various things sustaining her now short life, I moved closer. I leaned in and whispered, "Thank you." And, after a pause, "I'm sorry." I didn't know why, though I was acutely aware the moment demanded my apology.

A moment or two later, I made her two promises that I knew she needed to hear. They were the only things I could give her in this, our last moment together. I told her I would help take care of my father from wherever I was. As a final gift to her, my second promise was that I would at last do what she had urged me to do for decades: *move closer to God.*

The beauty was that it would be a gift from her to me.

I smiled for many reasons during those dark days. My mother was frugal, and all this happened during an airline price war, making it possible for me to fly out for the hospital, the funeral, and the internment. She also passed away during the weeks leading up to lent, so when it was time to deliver my second promise, church services were available daily.

Soulful reconnection carried me through my grief.

I saw versions of my mother in these services: prayerful, dedicated women who opened their hearts and arms while reciting the Our Father. They too had transcendent, peaceful, expressions while they sat, kneeled, and stood.

They too walked slowly, wore modest clothes, sported practical haircuts, intent only on one thing: receiving God whole-heartedly.

Just like her.

I missed her terribly.

To celebrate the best of her, and to embody what I was coming to believe, I arranged for our boys to be baptized. The church clerk informed me the only time they could accommodate this was after mass, *on Mother's Day.*

I set the phone down and inhaled deeply, moving towards the bright sunlit window. I stood in it and stilled. Eyes closed, I smiled with gratitude towards the heavens.

CHAPTER SIX

When in doubt, go inward.

The years surrounding my graduation were a blur; before it was a frantic race to the finish line that required monumental obsession. Some days I rose at 3 am to polish off another chapter or I curled up on the rug from exhaustion for a nap.

The time after graduation was surprisingly harder.

Fear ruled over me again. What if I'd wasted my time on a degree I'd never use? Did my husband and I really survive those years? Did I? Unsettledness prevailed as talk began of him possibly leaving his job. This would be a bigger move. Selling the house, packing up everything we own to move to another province, possibly another country. After a series of doors opening then closing, nothing happened. I was back at my old job because it was still the best place to work. Extra letters on a signature block and a better office made little difference.

When the dust of no change settled, we made it happen on our own and moved into a bigger home with a bigger yard on a lake. Perhaps it was an attempt to control our own situation in some way.

Getting settled took longer than I wanted. Maybe it was grief over my mother, and the worry I carried for my father that slowed me down. Casual trips to church and more meaningful moments of prayer helped. I said the rosary a few times and was surprised by how many verses remained in my heart; however, it was not enough. Whatever the reasons, everything felt chaotic.

True to my other promise I visited and helped with my father's care whenever I could, which happened about three times a year. During visits I reconnected with old friends, some of whom provided me with new insights and points of reflection.

What is it about first loves that leave a lasting impression? It had been decades since we'd seen each other in person, well before we both married, and we decided to meet up for a casual dinner.

It was early summer evening. Though the patio was offered, we chose indoors. It was a light-hearted reconnection over good food. We traded news of family and friends, careers, all the usual topics. A goodbye hug by the vehicles, keep in touch and blah blah blah. The event itself was of no consequence, how I felt much later however, *was*.

My mind simply couldn't settle. I went down memory lane, got trapped in it, and was unable to find the door out. I loved-hated every moment of it. I fell down the rabbit hole of what could have been had I stayed there. I imagined all the ways life might have been easier: I would have been more available to my parents as they aged, and stayed closer to some exceptionally good friends. I would have had a home in a workplace of twenty-five plus years with a pension, the way many of my graduating cohort did. I loved his sister, and mother, I wouldn't have lost them. My mind spun, spun, and spun some more. I felt terribly unseated. I wanted only to live in the imagined, over-glorified version of a life I concocted. I didn't want to face the arduous task of unpacking more boxes, feeling the immense pressure of having to anchor all four us.

I'm proud to say that even frantic and scattered, I hadn't lost all senses. This was happening for a reason, all of it, I knew that deep inside. I loved my husband and boys *more than anything*. Of that I was still certain.

Dizzy from my spiralling, I sat down in the spare room of our new home to gather my thoughts. It was a make-shift office with heaps of unsorted things everywhere. I looked out the window and stared at our lush lawn. My husband has always given intentional attention to grass. He aerates, fertilizes, and waters appropriately. He buys hose splitters and sets timers for rotation. He invests in good sprinklers. One year he made one by carefully drilling holes into an empty plastic bottle.

I heard him on the lawn tractor beyond the window, somewhere in the backyard. No, it wasn't the mower, it was that monstrosity of a dune buggy he built from scratch, partly for fun but also as a father-son project. He wanted them to know basic mechanics.

It got louder, then sped past my window. The three of them took turns circling our unfenced home. I glanced out and noticed my older son at the wheel, he was fourteen at the time; *a real speed demon that one*, I thought. My husband cheered him on. I heard his hearty laugh as my son floored it. There was pride in his futile and feigned bellows of caution. The unmistakable smell of exhaust, of *"fun"* as my husband called it, reached me.

I shut the window.

I shut down the ramblings in my head.

Slam!

Enough!

I fired up the trusty Hewlett Parkard. (How it survived this long was beyond comprehension.) I searched again, channeling the same fury I used to find my PhD program, but this was different. This time, I was doing what I *least* wanted to do. What I had avoided doing.

I wasn't looking for a way out of my current life. I was looking for a way back in.

I was looking for help.

CHAPTER SEVEN

The truest measure of strength is vulnerability.

W ithin days I began unpacking my needs with a therapist in Toronto. She was exceptionally skilled, her voice calm and kind. She asked what I was looking for, and the sincerity in her voice brought me to tears. I told her I didn't know.

Our chemistry felt right; so, despite the three provinces and two time zones between us, we committed to weekly appointments.

I didn't know then that her voice would be my beacon in some very dark days to come.

Neither of us knew that by putting our best into this work, we would slowly bring me the rest of the way to the other side, where pain and loneliness were behind me. Neither of us knew that our work would span several years.

Time stood still for one hour every week. During sessions I allowed myself to pause for the first time I could remember. I allowed myself to feel, really and truly feel.

One day she asked what life had been like when I first arrived in Canada. My head ached instantly, then there was fuzziness. I yawned and tuned her out. I told her this, and she assured me this was a natural response.

The following week, after much thought I addressed it full on. I let her in on my thirteen-year-old self and how cold and strained my world had been. I let her in on all the deep wells of loneliness that lived inside me, untouched, unvisited, and how I hated their very existence.

As I spoke, I grabbed my Sherpa fleece blanket and wrapped it tightly around my upper body, curling myself up so I could hug my knees. My tissue was two-ply. I used three at a time and made a small mountain of them before the end of that call.

As the words and feeling poured from me, I stared out the window at the thinning trees. They barely moved in the strong wind. I envied them, I longed for their *rootedness*.

For me, therapy was about digging deep, searching for the biggest bleeders. It felt like we were airing out wounds, seeking them out and sewing up gaping ones. Each and every one, small and large. With care, with caution, with tenderness. The work was difficult. It was excruciating, and the pain seemed relentless. I prayed. I outright pleaded. I begged God for peace in my heart. I begged for a life that no longer hurt. At times when alone in the house, I screamed at the high heavens to listen to me.

"Listen to me!"

Perhaps it was from the urgent release of emotions and prayers that somewhere deep within me, a very gentle healing began.

I got strong enough to talk about the biggest source of my heartache: abandonment.

We talked about the years without my mother. I told her that back then there was always a radio playing, and how I took refuge in the sad songs of The Carpenters, Barry Manilow, and a country ballad called "Don't Cry Joni" which was a sad one about a girl who left a man for his best friend. I knew and sang every lyric. I told her of my love for fish sauce, how I doused every meal with it before my first taste because that salty concoction comforted me.

After that session, I listened to Karen Carpenter's "Caught Between Goodbye and I Love You" for the first time since my childhood because I could finally face it. Her piercing lyrics made me pause, sinking in deeper, knowing her own life had been a tragedy. I leaned my back on a kitchen wall and slid down slowly before I crouched inward. I needed to release more emotions that emerged, so I did. At the completion of two more songs, I rose to my feet, dusted off, and faced the day with a lightness I hadn't felt in years.

In another session I told her of the old lady who came weekly to do our laundry. She was a permanent structure in our home in Manila, regardless of how often we moved. She had thin grey hair that was held back with a giant clip, and never removed her large squarish glasses. I told my therapist about how I found this lady weeping one day as she ironed the collar of my father's striped shirt.

I asked her why she cried, and she said she was crying for us, that she was deeply sad and angry for us, three children left behind by their mother. She couldn't understand how any mother could do that, be away from us for that long. She had children of her own whom she talked of often.

I told my therapist how I don't remember crying at all back then, even when it shattered my heart to pieces to watch this slightly crooked woman, so dear to my heart, cry for *me*. That was me then though, broken innards, yet no visible tears.

My mother would later tell me that before she left Canada she'd pleaded with that dear lady to stay with her remaining children, "*no matter what.*"

This selfless caring soul passed away several years after we left. I didn't know, nor did I fully comprehend, the extent of her commitment. I don't remember saying goodbye to her when we left, I'm certain I never thanked her.

I told her how relatives frequented our home. After my mother left, my older cousin who'd been with us a while, took a prominent role in our lives. He was in his mid-twenties. He drove us to school, dragged us out to the park, taught us how to cook and wash dishes. When we had money to spend, he took us shopping for toys and colouring books. He was kind.

I told her of my favourite Tagalog song: "Dahil sa'yo, nais kong mabuhay..." *Because of you, I want to live.*

I sang that song often, and one day he stifled his laughter when I couldn't reach the highest note, so I screamed it in the pitch one uses when faced with vermin. Or snakes.

It was he who sat us down one afternoon on the front porch to tell us our grandfather had passed away; our father wouldn't be home that night, he'd said. His voice cracked a little, his eyes wandered away for a moment as if that movement would set a tear aside. He softly reassured us we'd leave for Pangasinan, my father's home province, six hours away. We'd leave in the morning, he said gently.

It was he who had birthday cakes ready with our names on them when our father wouldn't be home.

He was always there.

I never thanked him either.

All the hard things came up in session. This included the break-up I endured in my teens and the devastation of being so readily replaced. I spoke of the salt to injury of seeing my "replacement", the girl with long legs whose name made me cringe.

When it came to discussing my parents, therapy got even harder; however, I loved that for the first time in my life, I had the safety, permission, and tools to feel it all.

I was *outraged.*

The choices surrounding our immigration infuriated me. In a conversation with my father, well after my mother passed away, he mentioned that we were all—*the entire family*—set to leave for Canada together. *Together.* It had all been set, papers and all, he said.

This stunned me. When I was young and hounded him, I was told we were waiting for something, implying it was something out of our control. I asked my father why we didn't all go then, and he casually said they (more like *he*) decided one of them with an income would be better, even if we had to be apart. So, this afforded him the chance to climb the corporate ladder and send money. He was proud of his career achievement; he started as chemist in the lab and rose to be vice president. How lovely for *him.*

Our lives were ripped apart for money and status. My childhood, my teenage years, the person I had to become, *the survivor* I had to be to win every fight, big and small, in all areas of my life, was about *bullshit.* Without admitting it, he had just revealed to me that it was really about his ego.

Emotions were both overwhelming and exhausting during my sessions. Realizations took days—even weeks—to process, and I wanted to discontinue therapy. Every so often I would consider it, and I even tried, but I knew there was no going back. There were no steps to retrace, no "normal" to restore because my starting point was *hell*. Whoever I was before this journey was worlds away from all right, I knew that much. So, there was no other possible route than through it. One way or another I stayed the gruelling, gut twisting course. I kept showing up.

When the anger fizzled, grief lay beneath.

Hello hidden pools of sadness. I dove deep and bathed in them. I found what would and could never be: the sea of lost things, of things meant for me that lost their way. The nurturing, believing, and love-filled hugs I needed as a child that never came. The celebration of a good grade, my glorious love of colour, the dimple on my left cheek I didn't know I had until someone pointed it out to me in high school, the courage of my eye contact, and my knack for making strangers feel at ease. Lost forever was the voice of my mother, and the way she said my name. Her dated, unflattering clothes, her valiant effort at curls, the rhythm of her rosary praying whisperings. The mother I never really got to know and never could now. The parent asserting that I wasn't lucky to marry a good man, but that he was lucky to have me. The way parents should.

The beauty of grief is in moving through it, and then leaving it behind.

My therapist assured me that in healing, nothing really changes, but everything changes. Once we talk about the unmentionable yet unforgettable, we open the path for what is next.

CHAPTER EIGHT

Tears have many faces.

I got better at travelling back and forth, past to present, feelings and all. Sometimes the story would get trapped in my throat and I needed a moment to gather myself, but that happened less and less. I didn't know how much my compressed feelings had held me back, especially when it came to being a mom.

My therapist reassured me again. She told me that children have a knack for forgiving when parents relate to them in a genuine and kind way. I experienced a remarkable internal shift. I was more tolerant. It was as if I finally awoke to the life I worked so hard to build.

I remember a sunny spring day. Half the ice on our driveway had melted, the shady areas weren't yet clear. My younger son was close to finishing eighth grade. He'd always been athletic. He came to me that morning and asked for an outdoor basketball hoop. They were several hundred dollars, I found out.

My memories of the Philippines emerged, and I could see my older brother, his arm around a basketball, taking it wherever he went. I could also see dark haired boys, sweat stained shirts discarded to the side, dusty feet on worn flip flops, gathered under a rusty loop of rebar, passing, yelling, and vying, having the time of their lives.

Money was tight then, but I didn't care. My husband disagreed, deeming this hoop an unnecessary purchase. He didn't want to budge. I showed him a flyer with it on sale. He looked up from it and said, "His life isn't going to change if we get this for him."

His ignorance on such matters amused me. I respectfully held in my laughter and said, "You watch."

Two days later, father and son added the finishing touch of an NBA tri-coloured net.

Our son lived under the hoop the entire summer. He and his friends would be out there instead of in the basement. It became a reason to gather. This would lead to them asking for rides to play at the local gym. One friend would invite my son to join him after school in ninth grade, which would lead to the moment my son met the coach for the first time. This coach would pull him aside, inform him that he had plans for him, and later make him a starter on the team. By tenth grade my son would be pushed up to the senior team where he would also be a starter. He would play in provincials. He would make the free shot that would win a tournament. He would receive the Rookie of the Year award. In senior grades he would be MVP two years in a row. He would make an elite competitive team, on one occasion he'd be referred to as the best shooter on the court, and be scouted for a varsity team upon graduating. He would stand six foot four inches tall, and it would bring us so much joy and pride to see him own the courts.

I shudder to think of how different life would have been had my past been too painful to visit. This beautiful, passionate, double-dimpled, self-driven boy would never have been heard.

I also connected better with my older son.

I remember a day I came home at noon. Little things would occasionally trigger me at work. There were giant ones that day and I had to leave. I pulled into the driveway and noticed my son's car. Home for lunch, I deduced. As I came in the front door, he popped his head out from behind the door at the bottom of the stairs. He looked up at me and said, "Mom, I know what I want to do with my life! I want to be a mechanical engineer!"

He had two years left of high school, and in that moment, hearing the conviction of his voice, I was steadied and grounded in the present. Something about emotional rawness opened me up to all things, and as I gazed at his determined long-lashed eyes, I was swept away by their beauty.

It's as if I saw him for the first time, and my mind travelled to all the moments he was fixing and building. We didn't allow toy guns, so he made a 3D version from computer paper and tape, complete with a scope and some movable parts. He used to lay on the rug, head on the ground, staring at the movements of his Hot Wheels. He built Legos designed for nine-year-olds at three and a half. He built complex Bionicles, a more sophisticated version of Lego, before he could read.

My pause brought him to say, "I can do it you know!"

I cleared my throat and told him, with all my heart, "Oh wow, of course you can! It's a perfect fit for you. I'm so proud of you for figuring this out so early! Damn kiddo!"

He smiled, beamed, and went back to his chicken flavoured Ichiban.

From there I walked to our bedroom, entered the small walk-in closet, and broke down. Oddly enough, the emotions from my day at work primed me to embrace the joy and pride of having been blessed with a larger-than-life first born. He always had so much passion and gusto, blessed with the imagination to make all things happen. *God, he deserves this path. He was made for it. Heavenly Father, universe, please give this to him.*

Out of nowhere came a flashback of my own post-secondary plans. Before I was admitted into the social work program, I had to write an in-person essay about why I believed I was suited for it. It was an enormous gym with easily three hundred or more other applicants. I did what I could, but by the time I got back to the house several hours later, self-doubt won. When I entered our home, my father was in the kitchen finishing a call. As he replaced the black receiver back on the wall, he saw my tears and asked what was wrong. I told him I was certain I bombed the entrance paper.

He told me it was my fault because I'd been too busy doing "goodness knows whatever else other than studying."

I locked myself in my room for hours after, his harsh words stinging deeply.

When I returned to my joyous son in the moment at hand, I was grateful for feelings. More importantly, I was grateful for my ability to believe in him, in that moment, and that he felt my faith in him.

My son would, for the first time in his life, take his grades seriously. He would make the honour roll and stand proudly at awards night among a disproportionately small group. He would receive the acceptance letter for aerospace engineering, the program in his university of choice. He would earn various scholarships. In the summers he would power a standard bicycle and buy and repair a series of dirt bikes. He would ride the hell out of them and return when the only things clean were his teeth. He would receive his bachelor's degree and iron ring. He would decide on the path of combat engineer, something he commits to wholeheartedly, with intense physical training and mental resolve. To wait out the recruiting process, he would train to fight wildfires. He would score higher than the national average in his fitness level and would be hired on the spot during an initial phone call. He is grit, tenacity, and iron will, with the gentlest heart.

CHAPTER NINE

Love and loss are the markings of a life well lived.

As therapy continued, my lone, long buried voice became clearer. I was on the phone with my father, and he was ornery. We were talking about something critical, and he refused to listen. He stood his ground and then dismissed me. I raised my voice. To this he yelled, "Now YOU listen to ME, OR ELSE!" A threatening statement that usually caused us to submit and scatter. This phrase haunted my childhood memories, they were his go-to words, his final assertion of power that ended all arguments.

I responded, "Or else WHAT? You'll kick me out of the house? I HAVE MY OWN HOUSE!"

He hung up.

A couple hours later I called back to make peace. He was softer then and said, "I'm your father, I deserve respect."

"Yes," I responded. "I'm your daughter and I deserve it too."

He agreed.

There were a few more arguments, but our chats went slightly better after that.

Several months later, on Halloween night, the boys and I were out with another family. We drove in two cars, convoy style, hitting the good neighbourhoods "for the best loot!" the kids told us. While I drove, my phone dinged with an email.

My father took a little fall. He was fine but later felt unwell. My brother took him to the ER, and within a short time he slipped into a coma. It wasn't good.

Again, come.

To say goodbye.

Flight. Rental car. Drive to the hospital.

I was alone again with my parent, in the same unit. I held one of his hands between two of mine. His felt surprisingly warm, just as my mother's had seemed when I held hers near the end. There were no machines or tubes attached to him. He lay in a small, dark, windowless room, and the certainty of what was happening hit me. He would die. Soon. The staff knew it, so much so that they weren't wasting anything on him. Their '*he's hopeless*' approach infuriated me. That passed quickly when I fully understood his situation was exactly that: without hope.

I found myself in a quick conversation with God: *Thank you. Thank you for not taking him back then in the Philippines when he was my entire life, the only parent I had left to love. Thank you for letting him remain the singular force to protect us and keep us safe. His strong voice, his face, they tethered me; my life was sparse of many things, but he had been my everything.*

Thank you, Lord. If you must take him from me, thank you for taking him now, when I'm perfectly capable of protecting myself no matter what, and surrounded by much love.

I shuddered at what would have happened if he'd died back then.

Our last conversation was another argument. Our final words were harsh. I hated myself for fighting him so much in the last months leading to this moment. I squeezed his hand and listened to his steady breathing.

Despite his flaws, he was a man of courage and determination, whose strength inspired me to win necessary battles out in the world. Shortly after we'd arrived in Canada he invested at a bad time and lost all his money. Years later, he ventured into work that taught him how to make it. At seventy-five he earned his Certified Financial Planner certificate, and at eighty-nine, he died a comfortable man.

I spoke to him unsteadily, but with the intention of setting his heart at peace. *Oh, how I hope you can hear me*, I thought. I gripped his hand, and I asked him to squeeze if he knew I was there. There was a slight but definite tensing of his hand. I felt it. I felt him listening. I wasted no time and apologized from heart. I thanked him for the better life he afforded us; it was worth it I told him, the decision to come to this country, and I was sorry about all things he too had left behind, the losses he endured that I'd never know about. His own pain.

I told him in no uncertain terms that my heart was breaking that he was leaving me and that I loved him so very much. That I would love him always.

Then I begged forgiveness for my part in our fights. Just in case he was troubled, I told him I understood his stance. I told him none of that mattered, that it never did, that he must go in peace knowing he'd done all he could for us. For me. Because he had. *He surely and dearly had,* I told him firmly.

When I left the room, my brother nudged me towards a less busy part of the hallway.

He told me that in my father's final moments, he said he didn't like how things had been left between him and I. He wanted me to know that he regretted that deeply, and that he always understood why I fought him so hard.

I stilled, nodded, and stood quietly, listening. I accepted these words with thanks.

I walked down the hall slowly, looking for a private place where I could really and truly fall apart.

I found a washroom stall.

I walked in and locked it. I sat on the toilet.

Alone with the stench of urine and bleach, I allowed my heart to shatter into a million pieces.

CHAPTER TEN

More is hidden than is visible.

Several changes happened after my father's passing, including leaving military life and moving back to Ontario. Everything felt, and in fact *was,* entirely different. The work with my therapist had slowly changed me. Between that and my grief, I found myself acutely aware and unable to tolerate vagueness or untruths. It was time to deal with a central part of my life.

My marriage.

I could, for the first time, allow inner thoughts to become words. Did I marry him to get as far away as possible from the pain of my family experiences? Was I so desperate for an alternative life that I rushed through the first open door, slamming it shut behind me, double bolting and barring it? Or was it perhaps because he was the first man who didn't run when I brought up commitment? Had I known what military life was really like, would I have made different choices?

I don't know what set it off, but fury followed my reflection.

He married *me* to have a personal, private therapist at the ready. I initiated every deep conversation and pushed it forward. I detested the pursuing, the demanding, the pleading for closeness. I detested that robot-like stance he took, never mastering the 'leave work at work' concept.

I hated that the weight of our marriage itself rested squarely upon my shoulders, and he left me to carry it all.

What I detested most was that I didn't catch on early enough to put a stop to that entire dynamic.

And then, one day, I did.

We were in the living room and I was folding laundry. While discussing his parents, it came up that he and his mother had a conversation shortly before our wedding, some twenty years before. She'd said, "You know your children will be brown, right?" To which he responded, "Mum, do you *hear* yourself?"

He never saw the point of sharing this with me, understandably, but he really should have. He should have because keeping this from me left me vulnerable.

My husband's relationship with his parents was also complex. They weren't close. What made me drop the stained cotton t-shirt, what left me fuming, was the picture of our early years together. This tidbit he just revealed shed light on something critical. Things started to make sense.

His parents visited us often, regardless of my feelings on the matter. While they weren't keen on brown-skinned folks, they had, apparently, no qualms about using one, *this* one, *their son's wife*, to act as bridge to their son. She was a therapist after all. Perhaps there was even some underlying assumptions about dutiful, subservient Asian women.

They used me. They capitalized on my kindness and eagerness to please. All those hours of shallow conversation that demanded my listening ear, all the veiled criticism of anything and everything from my choice of home décor to how I salted my food. The constant calling of my name. (I loathed hearing it after a while). The endless one-way dialogue they pulled me into no matter how busy I was, which they couldn't miss because I was managing the household and their grandchildren right in front of them!

Then I found another deeper level of clarity: my husband used me as his buffer when they were around.

This stunned me.

Breathe. Just breathe, I thought to myself.

Emotions welled up and my head began to ache. The frustration, anger, and disgust were too much so I let the dam burst. "How DARE you let this happen," I told him. "How could you do this to ME! You are *supposed* to protect me! You are *supposed* to fight for me, you are supposed to stand *with* me! I AM A GODDAMN human being! You vowed to *love* me! How the hell can you do this to the one person who has stood by you all this time, and cared for you and the children you don't have time to raise! What in the goddamn HELL? How did YOUR relationship issues become my *burden to carry too?*"

This wasn't the first time I'd voiced distaste of his general absences, so I kept going. "Even when you're here, you're not," I yelled. Out came the built-up resentment for having to pull us closer. I unburdened, through tears of rage, releasing it all, allowing it to flow out, not thinking or caring one tiny bit about whether or not he deserved it.

I didn't CARE.

He stood still. Speechless.

I didn't know what to expect so I braced for a verbal attack, maybe accusations like 'well, I told you, you didn't have to sit there and listen,' or 'I asked if you were okay with them coming and you kept saying sure.' I mentally retrieved more evidence, certain that this was another time I'd be minimize or ignored. Or dismissed. Echos of my childhood loomed. I felt a chill. I crossed my arms for warmth; I reached for the nearby Sherpa blanket —I had many—stepping on the laundry pile to grasp it with both hands.

Aloneness.

Invisibility.

An irritant.

He stood behind our grey sofa, looking down at the top part of it without seeing it. His usually strong and assured stance was gone. My emotion fizzed a little, perhaps because the man before me was utterly lost for words.

His shoulders slumped. He was deep in thought, as if he too was replaying the years and moments in his mind. Still no words.

Then his expression changed. Eyes widened. Neck muscles tensed. The small shadowy line between his brows deepened. Jaw tightened. Was that anger or confusion on his face? Was it shame? Regret?

No, it was sadness. Deep and utter sadness.

One more thought emerged from the well of my hurts: *these truths broke him too.*

I will never forget the grace with which he handled that moment.

First, he shook his head, then he paused. He had allowed all my thoughts their warranted airtime. He received every one of them, never once interrupting. No excuses. No weapons. No defensive hand gestures. No backing away, no wincing, no leaving.

He let my heart bleed out its ache.

He listened. He accepted blame. He owned every misdeed and apologized with sincerity. I knew that tone. He used it whenever he told the boys he loved them or was proud of them. He used it when he told me he loved me for the first time. He used it when he uttered our wedding vows, eyes firmly planted on mine.

He looked up. He stood tall. He offered firm and solid eye contact again, just as he did twenty years before at the altar.

He made a solemn promise that, from that moment on, there would be no more using, hiding, or abandoning.

He would keep that promise, this good man.

From then on, he fielded all the phone calls, and took time off work whenever his mother visited. Her and I had grown to love each other over the years, but I knew, beyond the shadow of a doubt, that what she really needed, what they both really needed, was their mother-son bond to solidify.

I would know from his actions, I'd be surer than anything in my life, I married the right man. The very best one.

From that I learned an especially important lesson about forgiveness: when faced with meaningful and wholehearted remorse, it can, in fact, be effortless.

CHAPTER ELEVEN

Perhaps the greatest luxury we can afford ourselves is to let go.

Forgiveness started to come easier. I learned to forgive my in-laws (my father-in-law passed away by then) because I too had sons. The idea of them escaping the realm of my love and understanding was unthinkable, and I didn't yet know how far I would go to keep our hearts close.

It got easier to visit my own family story then, as forgiveness and moving past hurts were becoming universal acts. I could use them in every aspect of my life. I was learning to forgive myself for all the things I had done. While there was still a lot of pain, good memories began to emerge.

Back in the Philippines, when we were nearing our departure to Canada, arrangements were made for us children to spend time with our grandparents in Cebu. I recall that my father and his father-in-law had issues of their own. Our visit was to be for several weeks. We were to board a plane, the aircraft itself merely a few feet away, and my father bid us farewell. I looked up at him and suddenly, emotions took over and I couldn't bear to leave him. I clung to him. He couldn't pry my arms off, though I don't remember him trying. I sobbed helplessly, uncontrollably, perhaps even shamelessly. This likely prompted my siblings to follow suit.

My father, for the first and only time in my life I can recall, caved. He held us all in closely, and very gently whispered into our hair, "It's all right. You don't have to go. You're staying." I'm not sure what wrath he endured from the force that was my grandfather. There would have been something. There always was with him. I loved that my father, in that moment, didn't care.

My next fond memory was earlier than that, while we were still all together in Manila. It was a ridiculously hot day. My mother took us to the supermarket, all six children, and it was blessedly air-conditioned. When we got to the checkout, she was short a few pesos and had to decide which items to exclude. It was likely an embarrassing moment for her. I only knew that there was something special on the belt, something I wanted and couldn't take my eyes off of. I was staring at it: Magnolia Ice Cream, a national treasure. When I heard we couldn't have all the items, my heart sank.

To all our surprise, my mother put back a handful of things and let us keep the luxurious, frozen delight. My practical, very-careful-with-money mother chose the treat. As we piled back in the car, there was an air of levity and excitement!

A moment in my teens also emerged. I was in high school, sitting in my bedroom with the door open, fighting with an old typewriter I found in the basement. I was saving for a better one. My father finally found work after his bankruptcy, though it required him to go on the road. He was nearing sixty by then, there were more greys and wrinkles than I remember noticing. He paused by my door and told me that while out of town, he saw a sign that brand new electric typewriters were on sale, and with any trade-in, they took fifty dollars off the price.

The old thing I worked on was quite heavy. The thought of him transferring it from trunk to store concerned me. He shook off my words, telling me not to worry, and I handed him some of my savings.

On his next trip he took the clunker with him and returned with a beautiful Smith Corona that came with a solid carrying case and a replaceable corrective cartridge. I knew money was tight for our family then, reserved only for essentials, but I'm certain he added some of theirs to get me that beauty. My money alone wouldn't have bought it. I carry that dear memory, that expression of love and the belief that I would use the machine to its fullest, in my heart.

As my therapy continued, I started to see my parents in a different light. I don't know all the trials and tribulations that come with immigrating with children. For my father it was later in life, and I was one of the six lives they contended with. Uniting third world views into a first world environment poses challenges under the best of circumstances, so it's no surprise that fear, anxiety, and over-protectiveness made their way into our home.

Slowly and surely, as I addressed each new memory that surfaced—good or bad—I felt a little bit lighter.

CHAPTER TWELVE

Blessed is the moment when past and present embrace.

Feeling better and being better was such a gradual process I didn't see it happen. What I did notice was that my mind could visit more and more stages of my life with ease. In finding my voice, I also found my feet; I could now walk away from or towards whatever I chose instead of side-stepping the landmines of my mind. I was also learning to trust my gut feeling, and even more so, I was learning to trust the universe. These shifts would change everything.

Not long after my mother passed away, an opportunity arose for me to sponsor a caregiver. My cousin who cared for us in the Philippines was now married and his wife was hoping to find employment in Canada. This would open the path for them and their daughter to have a good life here. I had young kids, I fit the criteria, I agreed. I didn't know that it would cost me hundreds of dollars, that it would be a laborious process, that it would last three years, and that it would take several more for them all to settle as a family in Canada.

When he finally arrived, I avoided him.

I avoided speaking to him, and though we hadn't been face-to-face in thirty-five years, I also avoided seeing him.

He was a definitive, pivotal connection to my pain-filled past. I was afraid all the progress I'd made in therapy would be for naught. I worried that he would look at me and see the little lost girl, playing with her pink tea set, squatting on the concrete terrace, singing sad songs.

What if sad me was all he saw when we met? If he did, then I'd be her all over again, trapped, numb. Again. I feared he'd remember the shaky girl he dropped off on her first day in a new school, tugging at the yellow skirt of her uniform, staring down at black patten shoes, looking up only to ask the security guard where the fifth graders go. It terrified me that meeting him would pull me back to aloneness and strand me there.

Full grown adult me—better me—fought against that fear, stood up, and decided it was time. He'd been in Canada almost two years.

An email led to a phone call that led to a scheduled dinner out. It was a four-hour drive through a thicket of Toronto traffic, so I opted for VIA Rail then the Go Train. *Let's see what fate has in store*, I thought as I looked up some old friends. Yes, they said, they'd make time to meet up when I was in town.

It was a trip that would change my life.

My cousin and his family arrived at the restaurant before me. When I walked into the dimly lit establishment, I clocked him after a casual glance around. There was no mistaking that slight frame with thick wavy hair! It was silver now, but as soon as he turned to face me, the familiarity of his features reached my heart. I didn't know I'd missed him terribly. A flood of emotion hit me all at once and suddenly I could smell salty humid air.

Those slightly angled shoulders had carried the burden of our well-being, and that he did it for five years as a young man was unfathomable. Never a harsh tone that I could recall; he was always kind.

He sat next to me. Across from us were his wife and daughter. There were many warm hugs and stories. His soft voice was painfully yet joyously familiar. No one else pronounced my name the way he did: "Eeleena." He eagerly listened as I shared about my life and showed off photos of my husband and children. He ordered pasta with a white sauce—the pleasant garlicky aroma wafted over my plump honey garlic wings, savoury and juicy the way Robinson chicken was before my mother left. Flavours danced in my mouth.

Now in his seventies, he was thin but in good health. His smile turned his face into a sea of wrinkles as he told me how he loved us like his own brother and sisters. I confirmed yes, I remember he was with our family well before my mother left. He rhymed off my school names and details about where we lived, all with fondness. It was a blessedly joyful reunion, a true slice of heaven.

At the end of the night, they surprised me with a beautiful, deep pink, authentic Kate Spade designer handbag with a matching pink wallet. It was a set I adored but wouldn't dream of spending money on. This was a small token of gratitude they said, for leading them to this life they now truly cherished.

He remembered my love of pink!

I trusted my gut and the universe by coming on this trip, and both delivered.

The powerful experience of seeing my cousin equaled the collective events that followed.

The various get-togethers over those few days are vivid even today:

> A dear friend from high school with whom I kept in touch through the years; I got her a job where I'd worked, and she organized a gathering of our old team thirty years later!

> Dinner with an old roommate who helped me through a few break-ups. He sings today, and his voice, the steady calming force during some turbulent times, sounds a little bit like home.

> I met with the only Filipina friend I made in northern Alberta, with whom my accent returned whenever we spoke. I never noticed of course, but my kids chided me. She was a fantastic cook; her meals back then had comforted me.

> And finally, a dear soul I hadn't seen in decades, someone I'd met during my time in the prairies. She had become a professional tarot card reader. True to her generosity and good nature she pulled out her deck, adeptly shuffled, and read them. Then, with mischievous eyes and her trademark broadly bright smile, she declared, "Oh, girlfriend. It's time for you to come out of that shell and spread your vibrant peacock fan." Bam! Hammer hits nail head. She remains one of my favourite people today.

These were some of the people I'd chosen, the kind folks who loved me like family when my own could not. These lovely characters were the external world I sought to create at age thirteen, and as I write this now, I'm stunned by a realization: I did it!

I dreamed of this in my childhood and teen years. I longed to be seen, valued and cherished. I ached for love and acceptance. Well, I'd found it. I found, in friendships, enough pocket-sized moments of closeness and intimacy to carry me through. These got me to the time and place I dared to hope for, the place where I arrived and am enveloped in love from a family of my very own.

I got by with a lot of help from my friends. I learned in this trip that they too received love and acceptance from me. Throughout the years I worried that I'd been a selfish 'taker'. This trip proved once again that my inner voice had been wrong.

It was as if I mended a frayed seam of my early life and trimmed off loose threads.

As I stood in line waiting to board the train, my rich blue Osprey backpack was slung over my left shoulder. It felt lighter. I felt buoyant but grounded. Trains screeched. Bright lights, arrows, and the subtle scent of locomotive fumes surrounded me. Someone walked past with a breakfast sandwich. I inhaled the aroma of bacon. I could see, smell, and feel everything.

I felt alive.

I was alive.

I hadn't felt that full, that magical, that rooted, for as long as I could remember!

CHAPTER THIRTEEN

Any moment can have the grandeur of a wondrous beginning.

That whirlwind trip was almost two years ago, and some big conversations followed it. I sat on a bar height stool pulled up against the brown speckled granite island, the same counter I had a loving conversation with my son years before. As I stared at it, I wondered why anyone would pay so much for dull beige with black spots. It always looked dirty and sad.

My husband walked past me to ready his brew. Seeing the back of his head tightened my throat. I watched his routine: Melitta cone, filter, grind beans, kettle on. When his cup was full and tailored, I asked him to join me.

It's time for you to spread your vibrant peacock fan filled my head. I didn't know what I wanted or needed to say, but what released were slow tears. I told him I'd been unhappy in this house. The boys had gone off to school, he worked on the other side of the city so much of my time was spent alone inside a structure that echoed. This house felt empty, and in it, so did I.

Maybe it felt a little like the Manila house. It did have similarities, but I hadn't noticed it before when the kids where there. He asked if it was the house itself. I said yes, that and the location. This was the best one available when we came on a house-hunting trip to Ottawa five years prior. We had little choice then. Now was a different story.

This loving man who detests change, who poured his heart and soul into adding a fence and finishing the basement, paused, then reluctantly agreed to consider other options.

Once again, the universe delivered. Several months later, the day before my birthday, my phone dinged with the notification of another new listing. I was up on the ladder painting the last bedroom. When I came down, I glanced at the four-inch screen. A quick text to our friend and agent confirmed that yes, indeed, it was horribly dated and will need a lot of work, but it has potential. That afternoon I drove by it. I surveilled from behind a mature cedar wall and held my breath. The photos didn't do it justice. I called our agent and asked her to get us in there to see it as soon as possible.

We saw it the next morning, made an offer the day after, and then she was ours. I joked that because we saw it the day I turned fifty-three, my husband bought me a house for a gift.

I sit in it now. It's a cozy oversized bungalow with natural elements, bright windows, rugs, and plush pillows. It's bursting with colour, all the artwork on the walls is borne of my hands. It's the largest home we've ever owned. My office faces the morning sun which shines upon me every day.

The previous owners had customized built-ins installed to make a professional grade craft room. It's simply magnificent! I'm surrounded by vibrant shades of pink, blue, orange, and yellow on all four walls. My pothos plant thrives here. As do I. I fondly named it my *Makeshop*.

My husband's commitment to being an exceptionally good man astounds me, and it warms my heart to see that our sons are following suit. Our boys came back home because it has a two-bedroom basement apartment, complete with a dishwasher and a theatre room. We also have the blessed addition of a significant other once in a while who is such a pleasure to be around.

There is unmistakable warmth and lightness in every square foot. There is ample 'crispy fish skin' since we are always stocked up on everyone's favourites. Often there are scents of something simmering, baking, or sizzling. Today it's bacon, a smell that should be bottled and marketed. My youngest and his girlfriend are meaningful about their meals. I hear them giggling and it's music for the soul. They always make extra. I'm sure a slice of cured pork awaits me.

My boys, now twenty and twenty-three, have a habit of astounding me with their goals, even more so with their commitment to them. They know we view them as the earth and sun, the moon and stars, the way every human deserves. I often say silent prayers of thanks, even for the pain, especially for it. Every single tear, every guttural heave, every piece of me I've lost or will never have. I also know something very deeply, truthfully, etched on my heart: *I would do it again, all of it, several times over, for these young men to stand as solidly and mightily as they do today.*

I look back and see how that trip to see people from my past, was the last curve that my life's trajectory needed. It seated me in the place I reached without knowing it. It was a mental "You are here" on a map. It's as if I saw my starting point, life in the two-storey, echoey house in Manila, to my glorious present day. What a journey it has been. I can't conceptualize the immeasurable distance between how both lives felt. Indeed, a lot will happen in five decades, but that world and the way I experienced living is several lifetimes away. I wouldn't have believed that it was conceivable, let alone possible, to get here, from there.

Today I launched my first psycho-educational courses online, in addition to the small virtual private practice I want to carry. The group electrifies me beyond what my body can process, so much so that I break up the day with frenzied physical activities to expend the build-up. I'm doing this with a business coach because I now know how little I know. I don't hesitate to ask and pay for help. I'm terrified of how desolate my existence and my soul would be without professionals.

When I think about my story, I no longer wonder how I arrived at this junction whole. I know now. *I* got me here. *I* own it. *I* did it by bringing whatever else I had to work with, whatever was left, to the table. One way or another, somehow, some place. Confused, heartbroken, terrified. I showed up anyway.

I showed up anyway.

I chose the book title before I knew what it was to be about. I thought it was about resilience and fortitude. It is, but it's many other things. It's the greatness of others who help us along the way, genuinely good folks who invest in us. Some are blood. Some are paid. Some are just there, doing their thing right next to us.

It's also about the greatness in the larger beyond that we know little about. I see now that greatness, the all-encompassing divine, the universe itself, always had my back. My mother would have called it God's work and I whole-heartedly agree. A laundry lady with a heart of gold. A well-placed cousin. The first young man who genuinely loved me. Kind acquaintances that turned into friends. The real deal of a man who vowed to love me until his dying breath. My cherished South African kindred soul. My skilled therapist, the only one who called me back. The lining up of events that led to a handful of cornerstone people, located in the same city, available when I planned that fateful trip. You, kind reader, who kept me company, and others like you whom I hope will be drawn to this enough to read it to this point.

I thank you from my deepest place. I'm honoured you have travelled along this far, and I dearly hope this book will serve your own journey forward. Please let me know either way. I wish only that it reached your soul because that's what I was speaking to.

With gratitude and joy, from the influence of the generation before and after me, I wish you well. May your path lead you to your best place. Perhaps it already has!

Acknowledgements

This book is about greatness, so I must mention as many greats as I can here. I hold my brothers, sisters, and their families in my heart, with only admiration and respect. The word family is such a beautiful thing, and I've been blessed to experience it broadly as life took me down many roads.

Some people enter our lives for good reasons, and I've learned not to question the how and why. FeViet Aplegren, you were my first real friend in Canada! Thank you for talking to me in eighth grade. Some noteworthy folks through my high school years were Colleen Woodruff, Gianna Scalcione, Beata Naemsch, Jennifer Desouza, Myra Santos, Marcia Daley, Haseena Hanuman, and Steve Ryan. (I still owe him for those floor tickets to the Rolling Stones. Beata and I still claim street cred for having gone!)

My Ryerson years are treasured because of Shelly Lair, Lynn Jaglall, Laura Cunningham, Andrew Gaiger, Michelle Lewis, Geoff Boisseau, and of course the amazing Jeff Cassidy. These are wondrous humans who had a way of making someone feel seen and special. I doubt I've ever thanked you, so I'll do that now. Thank you! No really, thank you.

Across the nation as we entered military life, standing in a league of their own are Heather and Paul Gautron. They were and will always be family. The years brought me marvellous ladies like Charmaine Imbeau, Allison Grover, Cindy Hamilton, Deb Livergood, Diana Garfield, Dana Charbonneau, Shelley Leduc, Melanie Matthews, Elsa DeLeeuw, Catherine Hansen, Kathy Thorneycroft, Irma Santiago, April Clements, Pat Rivard, Audrey McFarlane, Shayna Elliot, Joey Vap, and Chris Jutte. These are superb humans who selflessly gave to me without hesitation. I must highlight Pat and Keri Hutcheson, and Joe and Marie-Michele Siu, you will never be rid of me/us!

The best part of my master's degree was the lifelong friendships I made with the superstars Tache Hall, Charlene Cowling, and Nushina Mukhi. This was also around the time I met the legendary Lori Simeunovic (despite her fame she is always amazing Lori), and the gone but never forgotten Shawna Cogswell Young and Ann Marlow.

My doctoral years, oh my goodness, I would have succumbed to the weight of it all without the love and support of Brigette Krieg, Yasmin Dean, and Hieu Van Ngo. I survived it because of your company! The expertise, patience, and kindness of my then mentor Leslie Tutty is unparalleled; she dealt with me at my worst yet never fired me.

Present day, many of these amazing souls of different life stages are still in my life. I thank Sandra Priestley, Ashley Chandler, and Laurie Gagnier, fine ladies who move mountains with the work they do. I also salute all the inspiring ladies of my To Be Real! Group, if I named you here I'll lose my license, but know you are and will always be very special to me!

I am forever grateful to the gift from heaven named Rose Marie Donovan of Alliance Psychotherapy.

Alanna Rusnak, my mentor and publisher, made this book happen. I came to her with a vague idea, she very gently cleared the path for this all to emerge, seeing past the bullshit I thought I should write, to the book bursting to be written. I so looked forward to our meetings, always walking away feeling like I could conquer the world.

A big thank you to Liz & Jane Photography; I fell in love with what Liz did with light. Liz you were a pleasure to work with, I thank you for making this happen during crazy times.

Last and certainly not least, thank you Reagh. Thank you for fighting me to get to me, and for defeating my protests with the declaration of, "I know enough about you, and what I know I like." Eric and Adam, you light up my world beyond comprehension, you ARE, and always will be, my reasons for everything. It wouldn't surprise me if someday Adam designs a flying machine, Eric builds it with his bare hands, and Reagh flies us all in it. There'll be room for Maddy Skiffington too, always.

Thank you everyone, for your collective gifts, for all you've done to enrich the lives around you. You most certainly enriched mine.

Elena Sherwood received her BSW from Ryerson in Toronto, an MSW from the University of Manitoba, and a PhD from the University of Calgary. She has done much to further the study of Canadian military couples and is a peer-reviewed sole author in the Clinical Social Work Journal. With basic and advanced training in CBT, EMDR, and EFCT she has over thirty years of clinical expertise, maintaining a small practice to make room for her obsession with the word *real*. She ran two empowering Facebook groups called "To Be Real!" and grads are now fully invested in her ongoing group called "Keeping It Real". You'll find her hanging out in her favourite online places: "Being Real with That Therapist Chick"; her podcast, Dr Elena–That Therapist Chick; or blogging at dr-elena.com.

Mostly though, she's donned in denim coveralls playing with colour in all mediums: Cricut, 5D diamond painting, and upcycling are the top contenders, all approached with a mid-century-modern-boho flair. She lives in Greely, Ontario with her husband, her intermittently present sons, and her rescues (a kind-hearted shepherd/doberman and mean boss tabby).

Made in the USA
Monee, IL
25 August 2021